MOON FLIGHT ATLAS

DREAMS
OF SPACE
BEFORE APOLLO

DAVID JEFFERIS

CRABTREE
PUBLISHING COMPANY
WWW.CRABTREEBOOKS.COM

INTRODUCTION

In books and movies, our early ideas about how humans could travel in space included being shot to the Moon in a large cannon shell. In real life, Russian scientist Konstantin Tsiolkovsky began developing ideas on how rockets could be launched into space in the late 1800s, while from 1926 to 1941, American scientist Robert Goddard built a series of successful rockets. Later, German scientist Wernher von Braun spearheaded much of the U.S. space effort. Here, you can find out how the work of these and other space pioneers paved the way for the Apollo Moon landings.

🌳 Crabtree Publishing Company

www.crabtreebooks.com   1-800-387-7650

Copyright © **2019 CRABTREE PUBLISHING COMPANY**.
All rights reserved. No part of this publication may be reproduced, stored in a retrieval system or be transmitted in any form or by any means, electronic, mechanical, photocopying, recording, or otherwise, without the prior written permission of Crabtree Publishing Company.

Written and produced for Crabtree Publishing by:
David Jefferis

Technical advisor:
Mat Irvine FBIS (Fellow of the British Interplanetary Society)

Editors:
Mat Irvine, Ellen Roger

Proofreader:
Melissa Boyce

Prepress Technicians:
Mat Irvine, Ken Wright

Print Coordinator:
Katherine Berti

Acknowledgements
Acknowledgements
We wish to thank all those people who have helped to create this publication and provided images.

Individuals:
Chesley Bonestall
Randy Cridland
Mat Irvine
David Jefferis
Gavin Page/The Design Shop

Organizations:
Canadian Museum of Flight
Galileo Project/Rice University
NASA
Smithsonian National Air and Space Museum
Takom Models
The Observer, London

The right of David Jefferis to be identified as the Author of this work has been asserted by him in accordance with the Copyrights, Designs and Patents Act 1988.

Printed in the U.S.A./042019/CG20190215

Library and Archives Canada Cataloguing in Publication

Jefferis, David, author
        Dreams of space : before Apollo / David Jefferis.

(Moon flight atlas)
Includes index.
Issued in print and electronic formats.
ISBN 978-0-7787-5408-4 (hardcover).--
ISBN 978-0-7787-5417-6 (softcover).--
ISBN 978-1-4271-2212-4 (HTML)

        1. Space race--History--Juvenile literature. 2. Manned space flight--History--Juvenile literature. 3. Space flight to the moon--History--Juvenile literature. 4. Moon--Exploration--History--Juvenile literature. 5. Moon--Maps--Juvenile literature. I. Title.

TL788.5.J44 2019   j629.45009   C2018-905615-0
                                              C2018-905616-9

Library of Congress Cataloging-in-Publication Data

Names: Jefferis, David, author.
Title: Dreams of space : before Apollo / David Jefferis.
Description: New York, New York : Crabtree Publishing, [2019] | Series: Moon flight atlas | Includes index.
Identifiers: LCCN 2018060550 (print) | LCCN 2019000728 (ebook) | ISBN 9781427122124 (Electronic) | ISBN 9780778754084 (hardcover : alk. paper) | ISBN 9780778754176 (pbk. : alk. paper)
Subjects: LCSH: Space race--History--Juvenile literature. | Astronautics--History--Juvenile literature. | Manned space flight--History--Juvenile literature.
Classification: LCC TL788.5 (ebook) | LCC TL788.5 .J44 2019 (print) | DDC 629.45--dc23
LC record available at https://lccn.loc.gov/2018060550

MOON FLIGHT ATLAS

CONTENTS

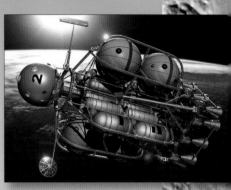

DREAMS OF SPACE

Seeing the Moon has always inspired people to want to go there, even if they had unrealistic ideas of how to get there.

⬆ Author Jules Verne's early Moon travelers were described as floating without gravity. Verne and Georges Méliès (*above right*) both used a large cannon shell to carry their astronauts.

??? How could we travel without rockets?

In the 1800s, science fiction writer Jules Verne described a super-powerful cannon that shot his explorers into space. It was not a very good idea. Without any steering or landing gear, such a trip would end in a crash landing.

Even so, the French filmmaker Georges Méliès used the idea (*above*) for his 1902 movie *A Trip to the Moon*.

??? How far away is the Moon?

The Moon is just "next door" as space distances go. It circles, or orbits, our world about 239,000 miles (385,000 km) away. The flight from Earth to the Moon took about three days during the **Apollo** missions of 1968 to 1972.

Earth's diameter is 7,926 miles (12,756 km)

The Moon's diameter is 2,159 miles (3,475 km)

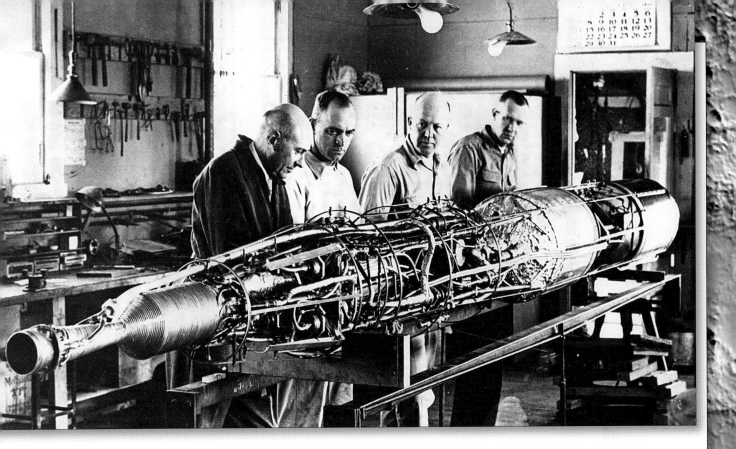

??? Who was Robert Goddard?

He was an American scientist who worked around the same time as Oberth. Few people took much notice of Goddard's work, yet it involved designing and building dozens of rockets, from 1926 to 1941.

Today, Goddard is viewed as one of the leaders of early rocket research.

→ *Goddard stands in the snow, next to a test rocket. He is holding the spidery metal stand that keeps the rocket steady before launch.*

??? What powered Goddard's rockets?

Goddard decided to use liquid fuels, as do most rockets built today. He successfully built and launched more than 30 rockets.

Goddard's rockets were not very fast by today's standards. But one hit a top speed of nearly 550 miles per hour (900 kph).

↑ Goddard (left) and his team at work on a liquid-fuel rocket in their engineering shop.

DEADLY MISSILE
FIRST ROCKET TO SPACE

The V-2 of the 1940s was first used as a weapon. But later, it became a space research tool.

Wernher von Braun

??? Who designed the V-2 rocket?

The V-2 was designed by Wernher von Brau. He led a team of scientists to create the deadly rocket for German forces in World War II. Many V-2s were fired against targets in Belgium and Britain. Each V-2 carried up to 1 ton (0.9 metric tons) of explosive in its nose cone.

When the war ended, von Braun and his rocket team were taken to the United States to continue their work.

??? What made the V-2 so advanced?

Von Braun brought together the sophisticated equipment needed for a successful large rocket. After the war, the ideas behind it could be developed even further.

The V-2 had a liquid-fuel system, much like Robert Goddard's rockets. For steering, it had two sets of rudders. Four of the rudders moved in the rocket motor's exhaust, four more were on the fins. The long, bullet-like shape allowed the V-2 to remain stable during high-speed flight.

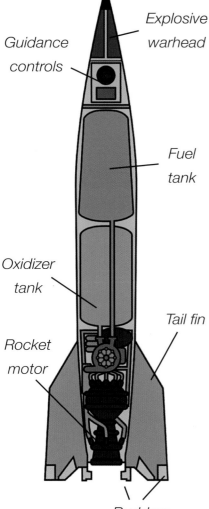

Guidance controls

Explosive warhead

Fuel tank

Oxidizer tank

Rocket motor

Tail fin

Rudders

⬆ **The V-2 had a fuel mixture of alcohol and water. This was burned with liquid oxygen (called the oxidizer) inside the motor to provide a huge blast of flaming power.**

A truck pulled the V-2. Fuel and supplies were carried separately.

⬇ The V-2 was a mobile weapon that could use a small launchpad. The rocket engine fired for about one minute.

Metal clamps kept the rocket in place

At a launch site, the carrier erected the V-2 to a vertical position

⬇ **Three V-2s being prepared for launch from a secret base.**

??? How fast could the V-2 travel?

After takeoff, a V-2 traveled upwards in a high arc for about 200 miles (320 km), before crashing and exploding. Its top speed was nearly 3,600 miles per hour (5,800 kph). In June 1944, a V-2 flew more than 62 miles (100 km) high, to reach the **edge of space**.

Wernher von Braun said the rocket would free humans from "...the chains of gravity which still tie us to this planet. It will open the gates of heaven."

One idea for a future V-2 included wings and a pilot

FROM IDEAS TO REALITY

Rocket engineers worked hard to turn dreams to reality. They were developing spacecraft that could take us to the Moon.

??? Did an early rocket fly to space?

Yes, during an eight-flight test series called Project Bumper. The base rocket was a converted V-2, on top of which was a smaller rocket, called a WAC Corporal. When the V-2's fuel ran out, the WAC Corporal took over to fly faster and farther. The highest flight in the Bumper series was in 1949, when a WAC Corporal hit a height of 244 miles (393 km) above ground.

↑ Cameras record the launch of a 1949 Project Bumper test flight.

??? What were planners aiming for in the future?

Technology in the late 1940s was still very simple by today's standards. Scientists and engineers worked constantly on plans for rockets that could one day make their dreams of space come true.

Among the best ideas were those published in the U.S. magazine *Colliers*. The winged launch rocket (*above right*) was a design that might fly to Earth **orbit**, carrying parts to build a huge, wheel-shaped space station.

⬆ This idea for a Moon ship had room for 30 or more people in its nose sphere. The whole ship would land tail-first.

??? What about Moon missions?

Scientists thought of the Moon as their target, although most believed a landing would not be possible until around 2000.

The rockets (*above and right*) were ideas for ships that could be built in orbit, then flown to the Moon when completed.

Designers thought big in those days, mocking up designs that might carry dozens of people. They would set up a Moon base, and stay for weeks at a time.

➔ Two ships land on the Moon, firing their rockets to slow for touchdown, just as Apollo missions would do years later.

CHALLENGE IN SPACE

Sputnik 1 is carefully adjusted before flight

The 1957 launch of Earth's first artificial satellite, Sputnik 1, started what became known as the Space Race.

??? What was Sputnik 1?

Sputnik 1 was the first spacecraft to orbit Earth. The Moon orbits around Earth, and is our planet's natural **satellite**. A spacecraft built to orbit Earth is called an artificial satellite. The launching of Sputnik 1 by the **Soviet Union** marked the beginning of the Space Race. This was a rivalry with the United States for dominance, or power, in space that lasted for more than 40 years.

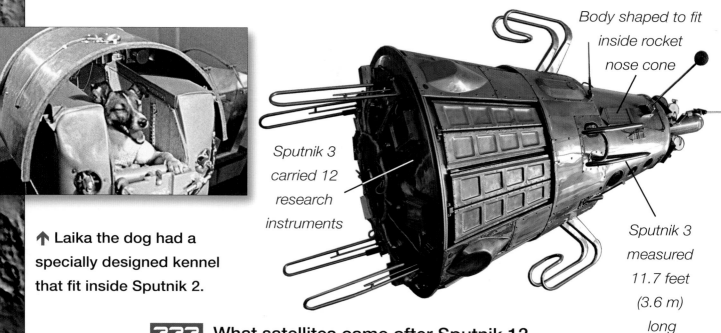

↑ Laika the dog had a specially designed kennel that fit inside Sputnik 2.

Body shaped to fit inside rocket nose cone

Sputnik 3 carried 12 research instruments

Sputnik 3 measured 11.7 feet (3.6 m) long

??? What satellites came after Sputnik 1?

Sputnik 1 was followed later in 1957 by Sputnik 2, which carried a dog named Laika. Sputnik 3 (*above*) was launched in May 1958, and weighed more than 1 ton (0.9 metric tons). The power of Soviet launch rockets was impressive, because Explorer 1, the first satellite launched by the United States, weighed less than 31 pounds (14 kg). The three Sputniks were a blow to American dreams of space dominance.

← Many early rockets were not very reliable. Here, an American Vanguard rocket is shown as it explodes into flames on the launchpad.

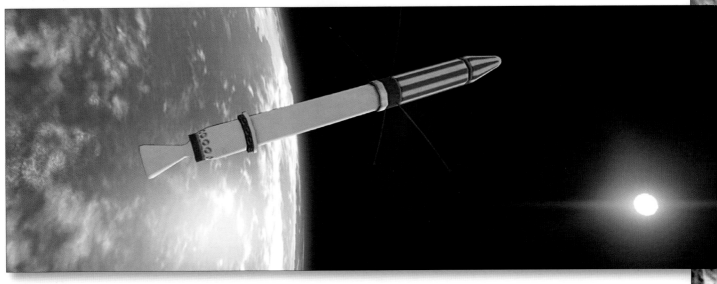

??? What was Explorer 1?

This was the first artificial satellite (*above*) launched by the United States in February 1958. Explorer 1 was far smaller than any of the three Sputniks, but its successful launch did prove that the Soviet Union had a competitor in space.

→ The Vanguard satellite was even smaller than Explorer 1. Soviet leaders laughed at its size, calling it a "grapefruit in space."

LEAVING OUR WORLD

In 1961, Yuri Gagarin became the first human in space. His achievement was a triumph for the Soviet Union.

↑ *Gagarin blasted off from Earth on April 12, 1961.*

??? Who was Yuri Gagarin?

Gagarin was one of 19 pilots chosen in 1960 to start training to be a cosmonaut, the word used by the Soviet Union for its space explorers.

Gagarin was only 5 feet 2 inches (1.57 m) tall, so he could fit fairly easily inside the small crew sphere of the Vostok spacecraft.

Air storage

Crew sphere

Equipment **module**

↑ Gagarin traveled in this Vostok 1 spacecraft.

Ejection hatch

??? How fast did Gagarin travel?

He completed a single orbit, moving at about 17,500 miles per hour (28,000 kph). The flight lasted 108 minutes. Gagarin (*right*) took off from the Baikonur Cosmodrome, a spaceport which is still used today. He used an ejector seat to leave the crew sphere in midair, before it hit the ground.

↑ Ham's space experience (*left*) helped prepare the way for human astronauts, such as Alan Shepard (*right*). His flight into space came a few months after that of Ham.

??? Who was Ham the chimpanzee?

Like Soviet researchers, the Americans also used test animals in the early days of space flight.

Ham the chimpanzee flew in a Mercury spacecraft in January 1961. During the 16-minute flight, he pushed levers in return for banana pellets. This was important, as it proved that completing a task was possible during a space flight.

> "...I saw for the first time how beautiful our planet is. Mankind, let us preserve and increase this beauty, and not destroy it!"
> *Yuri Gagarin, after his flight*

??? How did American space capsules return to Earth?

Unlike Soviet spacecraft, which came down on land, American spacecraft splashed down into the Atlantic Ocean. Helicopters first dropped divers in the water to ensure the capsule did not sink. Then, astronauts were airlifted to a ship that was waiting nearby.

→ A helicopter lifts a Mercury capsule out of the water. A bright-green dye was used to help the airlift team find the capsule, in case bad weather made visibility poor.

WINGS OR CAPSULE?

There were two basic design ideas for space engineers: rocket planes or simpler space capsules.

An X-15 on one of many research flights

??? What was the X-15?

This was a winged rocket plane used for high-speed research flights. Plans were made to convert the X-15 to go into Earth orbit. This might have been possible, but the Space Race meant that catching up with the Soviet Union was vital. The Mercury capsule took less time to build.

← John Glenn takes off, launched by an Atlas rocket from Cape Canaveral, Florida.

??? Who was the first American in space?

Alan Shepard made the first flight to the edge of space on May 5, 1961. This was called a suborbital mission, as his rocket did not reach orbit. Shepard's trip took about 15 minutes.

The first American to equal Yuri Gagarin's orbital flight was John Glenn, on February 20, 1962. His three orbits took four hours and 56 minutes. He landed and became a national hero.

Launch escape system to pull the capsule to safety in an emergency

↑ John Glenn, ready for flight in his Mercury capsule.

??? How big was a Mercury capsule?

It was tiny! There was just enough room for one, surrounded by 120 controls, 55 switches, and 35 levers. A Mercury capsule weighed 3,000 pounds (1,400 kg).

Window

← John Glenn's Mercury capsule was named Friendship 7.

→ The shape of the Mercury capsule resulted from much design and testing work.

Braking rockets

"Zero-G and I feel fine." *John Glenn on being weightless during his orbital flight. After returning from his successful flight, he said:* **"I don't know what you could say about a day in which you have seen four beautiful sunsets."**

GEMINI TWO-SEAT SPACECRAFT

The Gemini was another capsule design, looking much like a bigger version of the earlier Mercury spacecraft.

??? What was the design goal for Gemini?

Gemini was built to bridge the gap between the one-seat Mercury and the much bigger three-seat Apollo.

From 1964 to 1966, Gemini astronauts practiced many space maneuvers. Eventually, they not only matched the best Soviet achievements, but the United States became a leader in the Moon race.

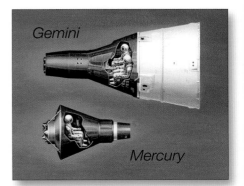

Gemini

Mercury

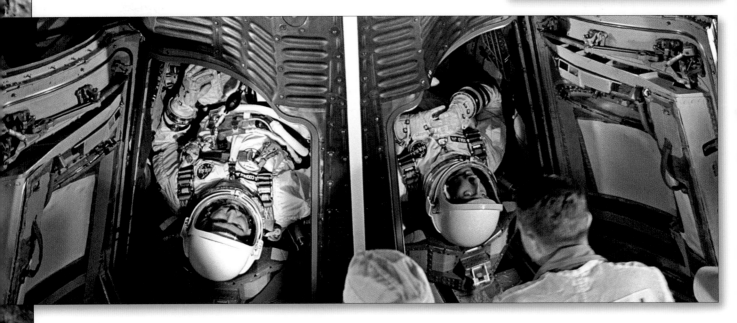

??? How many Gemini flights were there?

In all, there were 12 Gemini missions, the first two being test flights without astronauts on board. The crew sat in aircraft-style ejection seats, intended to blast them to safety if the Titan II launch rocket exploded. Some scientists believed that a Mercury-style launch escape system was safer. All Gemini launches went well, so the ejection seats were never used.

↑ Gordon "Gordo" Cooper (*left*) and Pete Conrad prepare for a week-long flight in Gemini 5.

Storage tanks

Storage for landing parachute

Command pilot in left seat, spacewalker in right seat

"I'm coming back in...and it's the saddest moment of my life."
Ed White, at the end of his spacewalk. He enjoyed it so much that he had to be ordered to get back inside.

Equipment module detaches before leaving orbit

Gas thrusters adjust angle of craft in space

↑ The Gemini spacecraft consisted of three main parts: the two-seat reentry capsule which linked to the rear equipment and service modules.

??? Who designed the Gemini?

The man responsible was Jim Chamberlin, a Canadian who had also worked on the Mercury capsule. Before that, he worked on an advanced jet fighter called the Avro Arrow.

Among Chamberlin's early ideas was for the Gemini to fly to the Moon with a small bug lander. An astronaut would climb in the bug and make a lone Moon landing.

??? Who was the first American spacewalker?

Edward White, during the Gemini 4 mission of June 1965. However, this was three months after the first-ever spacewalk, carried out by Soviet cosmonaut Alexei Leonov.

→ Ed White floats in space on his 20-minute space-walk, officially called an EVA (extravehicular activity).

TESTING FOR APOLLO

Gemini missions allowed astronauts to make maneuvers that would be needed when the bigger Apollo capsule was ready.

↑ Astronauts sit in a life-size Gemini model to check that the design works as planned.

??? How long did space tests last ?

The longest Gemini mission lasted nearly 14 days, with astronauts Frank Borman and Jim Lovell in 1965. They proved that humans could survive in space long enough to reach the Moon and back.

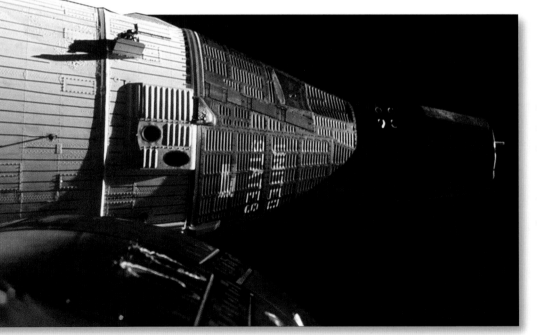

← Gemini 7 as seen from Gemini 6A. The two craft met in orbit to practice for Apollo missions.

??? How many astronauts flew on Gemini missions?

Sixteen astronauts were chosen as part of Project Gemini. Of these, the best known are Neil Armstrong and Edwin "Buzz" Aldrin, later to be the first humans on the Moon during the Apollo 11 flight in July 1969.

Armstrong was command pilot of Gemini 8, while Buzz Aldrin was pilot of Gemini 12. Armstrong was unusual in having flown the X-15 rocket plane, and for being a civilian instead of a navy or air force aviator.

??? What was the angry alligator?

This was a nickname given to the spacecraft (*above*) which was supposed to be a **docking** target for Gemini 9A.

Docking in space was an important maneuver for upcoming Apollo missions, which would need space linkups to be carried out without a hitch. However, the covering on an Agena target vehicle jammed half-open, so the docking had to be canceled. And that's when astronaut Thomas Stafford described it as "looking like an angry alligator."

↑ Docking with the angry alligator was a failure, but two later flights went well.

"We're rolling up and we can't turn anything off."
Neil Armstrong, with David Scott on board Gemini 8. Their capsule was out of control, saved by Armstrong's quick reaction in shutting down a faulty steering system.

??? How were astronauts picked up after splashdown in the ocean?

Like Mercury capsules, the Gemini came down in the ocean under large parachutes. After the splashdown, U.S. Navy divers came and attached a rubber collar (*right*) to make sure the craft did not sink. A helicopter then lifted the astronauts out of their capsule and took them to the ship waiting for them.

Dive team   *Flotation collar*

ROBOT EXPLORERS

Even before the Gemini missions, uncrewed space probes made several Moon flights. Their target was to collect as much lunar information as possible.

??? Why did Rangers crash into the Moon?

The American Ranger probes of 1961 to 1965 were aimed straight at the Moon. The plan was to take the first closeup pictures of the surface, before crashing into it. The first six Rangers failed, but number seven was lucky, and returned a whole set of closeups such as the one in the box below. In all, Ranger 7 sent more than 4,300 pictures, with Rangers 8 and 9 adding a further 13,000 to the total.

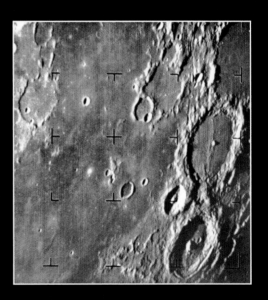

??? What did other robot missions achieve?

Mapping the Moon was essential for the planned Apollo missions. To do this, five Lunar Orbiters photographed the Moon, from 1966 to 1967. Their most important job was to survey possible landing sites.

This was before digital photography, so a Lunar Orbiter's two-lens camera used film, which was processed by a built-in laboratory. A scanner then converted the image into a form that could be sent to Earth by radio.

↑ Ranger 7 and an image it sent before hitting the Moon.

??? What were the Soviet Luna probes?

The Soviet Union was secretive about its Moon plans, mostly making announcements only when a mission succeeded. More than 24 Luna probes of different types were launched, many of which failed. But Luna 16 (*left*) succeeded in making a soft landing, then drilling into the lunar soil.

← Luna 16 landed in 1970, after the American Apollo 11 and 12 missions. But the probe made history by taking a small sample of Moon material, then returning it safely to Earth.

"These guys were operating right at the edge."
*Keith Cowing of **NASA**, talking about the team that worked on Lunar Orbiter missions*

??? How many Surveyor probes landed?

Seven Surveyor craft flew to the Moon from 1966 to 1968. One crashed and one was lost. The other five landed safely. Among other things, they made sure that the surface was firm enough to take the heavier Apollo LM (Lunar Module).

In 1969, the astronauts of Apollo 12 landed near Surveyor 3 and walked over to check its condition.

↑ Surveyor 3, photographed during the Apollo 12 mission. Before this, the Moon had been mapped by five Lunar Orbiters (*arrowed*).

READY FOR TAKEOFF?

During the 1960s, scientists and engineers developed the hardware and systems needed for rocket launches.

Early Mercury design being tested

??? What is a clean room?

It's a protected area, where no stray items are likely to get into a piece of machinery.

The Mercury capsule (*left*) is shown being assembled in an early clean room, its walls made of transparent plastic sheeting. These were sealed with tape, so dust or dirt could not enter from outside.

The technicians wore close-fitting surgical-style headgear, to avoid loose hairs falling into the capsule's delicate electronics.

← **The first Mercury capsule during manufacture in 1959.**

??? Could rockets be flown by air?

The Atlas launcher used for four crewed Mercury flights was 94 feet (29 m) long. Despite its length, the Atlas could just fit inside a U.S. Air Force C-133 cargo plane. Changes to the plane were needed for the job, such as replacing rear doors so that they opened wide enough.

↑ **Unloading an Atlas launcher from a C-133 transport.**

??? How were launches controlled?

Developing ground-control facilities to support flights was just as important as the spacecraft and astronauts.

The Mercury Control Center (*right*) was built from 1956 to 1958, and used until 1963. Its big feature was the wall map, with a model spacecraft that moved to show where the real spacecraft was at any time.

??? Why was a launch gantry needed?

At left is Launch Complex 14 at Cape Canaveral, Florida. Just before a launch, the red gantry rolled away from the rocket waiting for lift-off. Fold-up service decks (*arrowed*) were used for preflight checks, and also by astronauts as they walked to their waiting capsule.

↑ The Mercury Control Center, with giant wall map.

"…nothing was more exciting than working on the Mercury Program, because we were doing things for the first time. It was new."
Don Phillips, who worked on Project Mercury.

↑ Flight MA-9, the last Mercury mission, in May 1963.

??? What fuel did the Mercury launcher use?

This was a Redstone rocket, which carried a mixture of alcohol and water for fuel, with liquid oxygen as the oxidizer. These were similar to those used by Wernher von Braun's V-2 rocket of World War II (*see page 8*).

There are other types of fuel, including kerosene and liquid hydrogen. These were used successfully a few years later to power Wernher von Braun's mighty Moon rocket, the Saturn V.

→ Lift-off for a Mercury-Redstone. Like the Atlas launcher, the Redstone had been developed from a military missile.

MAPPING THE MOON

Astronomers have studied the Moon for hundreds of years.

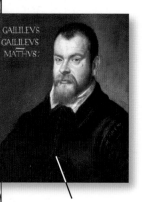

Galileo Galilei was born in Pisa, Italy

??? Who first mapped the Moon?

Observing and naming the Moon's features goes back for centuries. In 1609, Italian astronomer Galileo Galilei was one of the first people to make and use a telescope. It could magnify objects about 20 times, more than other instruments of the time. Galileo drew many sketches, including those above.

↑ Galileo showed how the Moon's appearance changes with the angle of sunlight.

??? How about other astronomers?

Others before and after Galileo also studied the Moon. Among earlier Moon watchers was the famed Italian artist and inventor Leonardo da Vinci.

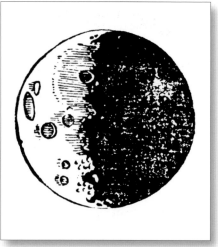

← Charles Malapert of Belgium made this sketch around 1619. A crater near the Moon's south pole is named after him.

→ Claude Mellan of France made artistic Moon studies such as this one, which he drew in the 1630s.

Ocean

Seas

Craters

Mountains

??? What are the Moon's main features?

The Moon has landforms that can be easily seen. Binoculars can show many of the details.

The Moon's seas and ocean are actually vast lava plains, formed billions of years ago.

Mountains were also formed when the Moon was young. Lunar mountains are mostly gently rounded, rather than the jagged peaks we see here on Earth.

Craters can be seen all over the Moon. They were made when space rocks collided with the surface.

??? Can we see the Moon's far side?

The Moon rotates in about the same time that it takes to orbit Earth, so we can only see the familiar "Man in the Moon" face. However, Apollo astronauts and space probes have seen and recorded the far side in detail.

The far side has mountains and craters, but no landform seas or oceans. In 2019, the Chinese Chang'e-4 probe landed there and provided details of the surface.

??? What are the Moon's vital statistics?

Here are some of the Moon's basic measurements:

Diameter	2,159 miles (3,475 km)
Distance from Earth	239,000 miles (385,000 km)
Gravity	One-sixth that of Earth
Length of day	29.5 Earth days
Temperature (day)	Up to 253 °Fahrenheit (123 °C)
Temperature (night)	Down to –387 °Fahrenheit (–253 °C)
Atmosphere	None, except for some trace gases

"It is a beautiful and delightful sight to behold the body of the Moon."
Galileo, in 1610. Of his research, he said:
"All truths are easy to understand once they are discovered; the point is to discover them."

TIMELINE

People and events that took space flight from being just a dream to real hardware used in the Space Race.

Before space flight

1609 Galileo Galilei (1564–1642) makes his first telescope and studies the Moon and other space objects.

1857 Konstantin Tsiolkovsky is born in Russia. He determines many of the basics for space flight.

1926 Robert Goddard launches the world's first liquid-fuel rocket.

1942 First launch of the V-2 rocket missile by German scientist Wernher von Braun. Later, his rocket team is taken to the United States.

Start of the Space Race

1957 The Soviet Union launches Sputnik 1 on October 4. In November, Sputnik 2 carries the dog Laika, the first animal in orbit.

1958 Explorer 1 is launched, becoming the first U.S. satellite.

1958 Founding of the U.S. space agency NASA (National Aeronautics and Space Administration).

1959 First flight of the X-15 rocket plane. Its highest flight reaches almost 67 miles (108 km).

← Ed White made the first American spacewalk from Gemini 4 in 1965. Photos of him were taken out of the capsule's open hatch by the command pilot, James McDivitt.

White's walk came about three months after a short spacewalk by Soviet cosmonaut Alexei Leonov.

1960 Wernher von Braun is placed in charge of U.S. space rocket development.

Humans in orbit

1961 On April 12, Yuri Gagarin becomes the first human in space, making a single orbit of Earth in the spacecraft Vostok 1.

1961 On May 5, Mercury spacecraft Freedom 7 carries Alan Shepard to the edge of space.

1961 On May 25, U.S. President John F. Kennedy asks Congress to commit to land a man on the Moon by the end of the 1960s, so launching Project Apollo.

1962 On February 20, Mercury Friendship 7 carries John Glenn into space, orbiting Earth three times.

1965 Cosmonaut Alexei Leonov carries out the first spacewalk, lasting about 12 minutes, outside the spacecraft Voskhod 2.

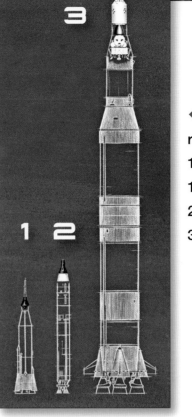

← American rockets of the 1960s included:
1 Mercury-Atlas
2 Gemini-Titan
3 Apollo-Saturn V

1966 Gemini 8 makes the first orbital docking with another spacecraft, an uncrewed Agena target vehicle.
     Gemini 9, 10, 11, and 12 also carry out successful missions.

Project Gemini

1965 Many space achievements are made using the Gemini spacecraft. The first crewed Gemini mission is flown by astronauts Virgil "Gus" Grissom and John Young, who fly for three orbits.
     In June, Ed White becomes the first U.S. astronaut to make a spacewalk.
     In December, Gemini 6A and 7 make the first space rendezvous. Gemini 7 goes on to fly for 206 orbits.

To the Moon

1967 First test flight of the huge Apollo Saturn V, to be used for flights to the Moon.

> **"Earth is the cradle of humanity but one cannot live in the cradle forever."**
> *Written by Russian Konstantin Tsiolkovsky in 1911. He determined many basics of space flight, such as orbital speeds and multi-stage rockets, even growing plants on board a spacecraft to provide food.*

GLOSSARY

Apollo The U.S. Moon-landing program, named after the Greek and Roman god of light and beauty

clean room A sealed area where dust and dirt cannot enter, that is used for the assembly of delicate machinery

docking Procedure in which two spacecraft approach each other, then link together. Several Gemini missions attempted to dock with an adapted Agena rocket stage, with some success.

edge of space Space has no real edge, as the atmosphere just gets thinner as you gain height. However, at 62 miles (100 km) high, there is little or no air, and this is known as the Karman line. Alan Shepard's Mercury flight of 1961 reached 116 miles (187 km).

gravity The force of attraction between objects, which varies according to size and distance. The Moon has six times less gravity than Earth, which is bigger, so a 132-pound (60 kg) weight on our world weighs just 22 pounds (10 kg) on the Moon. In orbit, objects (including astronauts) experience zero gravity (zero-g), or weightlessness.

module Section of a spacecraft that links with another. Modules may include the reentry and equipment modules of a Gemini capsule, or the two-part Apollo Lunar Module that landed on the Moon.

NASA National Air and Space Administration, the U.S. space agency

orbit The curving path that one space object takes around another

oxidizer One part of a liquid-fuel system, known together as propellants. The fuel (for example, alcohol) mixes with the oxidizer (for example, liquid

← Gemini 8 approaches an Agena target vehicle to dock with it. This went well, but problems with the capsule forced the mission to end early.

↑ A helicopter view of Alan Shepard as he is lifted from his Mercury capsule after splashdown.

oxygen) so it can burn in the rocket motor. There is no air in space, so both fuel and oxidizer are needed.

reentry Term for returning to Earth through the atmosphere

satellite A space object that orbits a bigger one. The Moon is Earth's natural satellite, while any orbiting spacecraft is an artificial satellite until it leaves orbit.

Soviet Union A group of 15 states, including Russia, that existed from 1922 to 1991. In the 1960s, the Soviet Union competed with the U.S. to try and win the Space Race to the Moon.

Sputnik A word used for several early Soviet satellites. It means "fellow traveler."

stage Part of a rocket, usually one of several used to boost it into space. It is often ejected and left behind when empty of fuel.

WEBFINDER

There is plenty of Internet information on the Moon, and even more on space exploration in general. Try these sites to start with, then you can go off on your own online explorations.

www.canada.ca/en/space-agency
Canada's space industry has a long history, and its robotic equipment works hard in orbit. Start here to find the whole story.

www.jpl.nasa.gov
The Jet Propulsion Laboratory has been involved in many space missions. The website has pages on current, past, future, and proposed flights— it's all fascinating stuff.

www.nasa.gov
The gold standard for space research, including Mercury, Gemini, and other NASA programs. Just use the search box to find out more.

https://spacenews.com
Excellent site that provides up-to-the-minute information. Space fans will want to visit often.

Have space launches been faked?
This question has been asked many times by people who think Apollo flights were a hoax.

Leaving aside other issues, the sheer number of people involved in a space launch makes any con trick a near-impossibility.

For example, 75,000 people at Cocoa Beach, Florida, watched John Glenn's launch. Eighteen ground stations around the world tracked the flight, and over 15,000 people were involved in recovery after splashdown.

INDEX

ABOUT THE AUTHOR

David Jefferis has written many information books on science and technology.

His works include a seminal series called World of the Future, as well as more than 40 science books for Crabtree Publishing.

David's merits include winning the London Times Educational Supplement Award and also Best Science Books of the Year.

At the time of the Apollo landings, he created news graphics for the international media, and has been a keen enthusiast for space flight and high tech ever since.

Follow David online at:
www.davidjefferis.com